282 Simple Ways to Face the Financial Crisis

THALIS P. COUTOUPIS

COPYRIGHT

282 Simple Ways to Face the Financial Crisis
© THALIS P. COUTOUPIS, 2013

English edition
ISBN: 978-1-910370-98-8

Digital edition
ISBN-ePub: 978-1-910370-49-0

Published by STERGIOU LIMITED
Suite A, 6 Honduras Street,
London EC1Y 0TH, United Kingdom
Web: www.stergioultd.com
email: eshop@stergioultd.com

I am not a politician
I am not a financier
I just have common sense
Thalis P. Coutoupis

"If you want to make him rich, don't give him more things, but
diminish his needs"
Epicouros – Greek philosopher (341-270 b. C.)

"Whatever does not kill me makes me stronger"
Friedrich Nitzsche (1844-1900)

"You must become the change you want to see in the world"
Mahatma Gandhi (1869-1948)

CONTENTS

Copyright 2

Foreword 6

INTRODUCTION 8

The problem and our responsibilities 8

Practical Manual for the Economic Crisis 11

We prevent, in order to have 11

TABLE OF EXPENSES 13

Reduction of Expenses 14

Shopping 15

Safety and Insurance 18

Marriages – Birthdays – Anniversaries 22

Vacations – Excursions – Travels 23

Diet 25

Work 26

Management of Debts 27

Clothing and Footwear 28

Repair of Damages 29

Small Business and Free Lancers 30

Hobbies 35

Electricity 35

Electronics and Gadgets 37

Social Expenses 38

Moving Around 40

Water 42

Children 43

Face and Body Care 47

Boats 49

House 49

Gambling 52

Telephone 53

Smoking 54

Health – Medicines 54

Province 56

Tips 57

Entertainment 57

Additional Income 60

Realty 61

Useless and Unnecessary Movable Things 62

Saving - Securing of Savings 64

Epilogue 66

Who is Thalis P. Coutoupis 67

FOREWORD

This book has been written mainly for the people who are financially weak, those who have been hurt in many ways brutally by the economic crisis. Even those though, who have escaped until know with only "scratches" or even those lucky ones well being can find useful elements in it.

It is a simple, but valuable tool. It does not contain hard to understand and complicated analysis nor prophecies nor wisdom nor magic solutions.

Its raw material is COMMON SENSE!

Its object is what tortures today the overwhelming majority of quite a few nations within the European Union and not only: THE ECONOMIC CRISIS. The crisis and how we may face it, not on a macroeconomic and political level, but on the everyday life of the individuals and their families in correlation with the family budget.

This "Practical Manual" records simple ways, in which, individual citizens can face the crisis in personal, family and professional level, in order to avoid major wounds.

Of course neither this book nor any other power can defuse or delete the crisis! What it is aiming at is to contribute to the maximum possible reduction of the unpleasant repercussions of crisis on any individual, family or business, suggesting simple practical every day ways.

It is certain that quite a few of the readers of this book know and practice already some of these 282 ways. It is also certain though that they will find among them some new, interesting, helpful ways, some of which may take them by surprise or even irritate them!...

The usefulness of this book lies in the fact that it gathered, organized and classified these 282 ways, in order to help the memory of its readers and also help them to organize their effort, so that they will manage to reduce their expenses in all the areas of their life and thus diminish the depth of the crisis bite on their body and their soul!

This Practical Manual is based on three axes:

- Reduction of expenses
- Increase of income
- Safeguarding of existing property of any kind

Its style may seem in some points "patronizing", but it has no such intention whatsoever. Please, consider that I am speaking to myself and I am sharing my thoughts with you!

Finally, this book is not meant for simple reading, but for APPLICATION! In the detailed table of contents, can each one find the area he is interested in and get some good ideas of how he can achieve the best possible management of his personal or/and family budget.

Thalis P. Coutoupis

P.S. I wish there would never be a need for me to write this book and for you to read it!...

INTRODUCTION

The problem and our responsibilities

We are facing a big, painful problem. If we want to face it effectively, we have before anything else to describe, define it and undertake which ever responsibilities, small or bigger, are attributable to each one. No solution is feasible, if the problem will not be composed and analyzed with sincerity and daring manliness and if its causes will not be understood.

To my humble opinion the economic problem is secondary. The primary problem, which generated the crisis, is political, moral and social. The tragic demolition of long-standing principles and values, which was dictated in a way by the political leaders, the media and other influential opinion leaders, was willingly adopted by the societies and did not only created the crisis, but in parallel is the main reason why the crisis is still here, after five years and there are no signs of when this will end!

The political problem is that most of the countries in EU were ruled by mediocre politicians, without commitment to a vision. As the great British historian, Amold Toynbee (1889-1875) has said though "Each people have the politicians it deserves"! And there lies the first and big responsibility of the European people, since we are the ones who have been choosing these inadequate political leaders for the last decades, the effort of whom was focused only in acquiring or maintaining power and all the material or immaterial dowry it brings to its holders.

This absolutely selfish philosophy did lead them to all sorts of illegal and unethical practices, corruption and patronage, both with the voters, the Media and the powerful business interests. Many of them have had on the top of their priorities to become rich and show off. Some rare exceptions did not have the necessary power to overwhelm the catastrophic scenery.

This attitude, except the primary damage it caused, had also another even worse repercussion, far more long term and difficult to annul, by giving the worst example to children and young people, for a painless, immediate and even illicit way of getting "here and now" mainly material goods or/and success! People are like small children. They do not listen to beautiful words. They just follow and mimic the example of the "status class", call them politicians, media, unionists, businessmen, artists, intellectuals, teachers and professors etc. Even more, when this example is painless, convenient, comfortable and pleasant!

The overall result is the contempt of all humanitarian principles, values and virtues, which lead to the financial crisis.

"WE" was crashed by "I" and unless this will be reversed, there is no hope!

Some people like to say they have no responsibility whatsoever for this crisis and they love to play the "victims" of bad politicians. That's a wrong subconscious self defense. We ALL collaborated to this crime and share a portion of responsibility, the first being that we are choosing and voting these incompetent leaders for decades now. It is true that not all of us bear the same portion of responsibility. Others are being held guilty for misdemeanors and others for crimes. Others ate a few smelts and other swallowed tones of lobsters. Of course there are again some extremely rare exceptions of citizens, who…did not have the opportunity to play dirty games, or some others, even less, who were adamantly honest and loyalists.

We did not vote on the grounds of meritocracy. We were and still are voting candidates superficially, based on their impressive TV persona, on being charming, on being famous athletes or artists, on having promised us to give job to us or to our children, on idealistic obsessions, on personal interests and not on the abilities, integrity and effectiveness of the candidates!

We over-consumed and over-borrowed, not according to our real needs and over and above of our income, just to show off!

We bribed public servants for illegal deeds or/and profits.

We did hide our income to avoid taxation.

If there is somebody, who has done NONE of the above sins, let him stand up and shout: I AM INNOCENT!

PRACTICAL MANUAL
FOR THE ECONOMIC CRISIS

We prevent, in order to have

If we adopt and apply this slogan, we have strong hopes to avoid total catastrophe or, at least, to diminish crisis' blows!

Before going into the core of this manual though, we need to agree on certain terms and meanings.

We don't despise savings of small scale, even those of ONE Euro. And that's because the repetitive wastes of small amounts leads to big total waste. In parallel even more important is that a permanent spirit of "saving" must prevail consistently in all our transactions and in our every day practice and life's attitude. That is savings not only on large sums, like rent, electricity, super-market, heating etc. but also on minimal amounts, like toothpaste, toilet paper etc.

All signs and analysts agree that the crisis is here to stay for a quite a long time and that things will be getting worse, until recovery, whenever this will come. So, there is still time to provide for to-morrow, so that we assure that crisis will hurt us and each one as lightly as possible. And if we do have some deposit, we should not spend it on consumerism, but keep it and if possible increase it.

This is the time, when

We don't buy and do whatever we like and wish, but only whatever we really need!

The reason why of this principle is simple: we lack today the cake we WANT for our enjoyment, in order to have tomorrow the bread we NEED for our survival.

Beside our effort to diminish expenses in a way that the quality of our life will be reduced as little as possible, our second goal must be the increase of our income and the safeguarding of what we possibly already have.

Most importantly we must rediscover the real meaning of our life and show:

- Composure
- Rationalism
- Patience
- Persistence
- Faith in our self
- Optimism
- Energy
- Creative imagination
- Boldness

Cutting a long story short the strategy of facing the crisis has three axes:

- Reduction of expenses
- Increase of income
- Safeguarding of possibly existing property of any kind

TABLE OF EXPENSES

The Bible for all those who really want to put in order their big, small or minimal budget is an organized Table of Expenses, which they must update every day, even with an expense of one Euro.

The Table of Expenses is the foundation of the effort to face the crisis. If we don't know, what and where we spend our money, we simply cannot manage our budget and organize any sort of saving. Actually petty cash and extra expenses constitute a very substantial yearly amount.

The Table of Expenses must be classified vertically in dates and horizontally in kind of expenses. Excel is the ideal tool for this exercise, offering automatic totals per date, per month and per category of expenses. People that are not comfortable with computers may make a Table, photocopy it and fill it in manually.

The categories of expenses vary from country to country, from family to family and from person to person. Nevertheless, here are some standard categories, more or less common to everybody:

- House rent and maintenance (Electricity, heating, water, telephone etc.)

- House aid (permanent or casual)

- Food and beverage (Super-market, drinks, butcher, greengrocer etc.)

- Transportation (Car, subway, bus, airplane, boat, taxi etc.)

- Clothes, shoes and accessories

- Children (School, toys, clothes, shoes, private lessons etc.)

- Entertainment (Vacations, excursions, theater, outing etc.)

- Social (Gifts, hospitality etc.)

- Personal (cigarettes, cosmetics, medicines, doctors etc.)

- Hobbies (Subscriptions etc.)

- Insurance (Home, car, health, life etc.)

- Various and extras

At the end of each month, we check each category whether it is within the budget we had defined or over it, and then we try next month to bring balance.

An effective practice for saving is to start from ZERO, when we design our initial budget of expenses, remembering we don't put down whatever we like and wish, but only whatever we REALLY NEED!

REDUCTION OF EXPENSES

Shopping

Market is and always was the big tempter! It is there, where we often exercise all of our repressed wishes and complexes, with hyperbolic, superfluous, meaningless and showing off buying, practicing fanatically the popular sport of over consumerism, cherishing as our god "life-style" with loans! If we don't forget these catastrophic habits IMMEDIATELY, if we will not change this mentality and our attitude of life, we have no hope and we will worth our fate!

Again, we start with the most important principle: "we don't buy and do whatever we like and wish, but only whatever we really need"! This rule is the core of the philosophy of this book and lies behind all and each one of the specific suggestions.

Don't go every now and then to the super-market! Nearly all super-market chains deliver their products at home provided the order is substantial. Choose the most economic chain, write down during the month your deficiencies in a piece of paper or in your computer and once per month, send a mail or a fax to the super-market, covering all your respective basic needs for the next month, which of course you know. You save labor, time and money, since according researches the "tourists" of super-markets spend 25-30% more than their list or their real needs.

Don't buy susceptible food in big quantities. Every household knows quite well its need from every kind, like meat, fish, milk, packaged food with short expiring date, vegetables etc. If you buy and stock more than the quantities you need, you will probably be forced to throw away food that expired or moldered. It is a big unacceptable waste and sin!

Try and buy unbranded goods. Sometimes they are of a better quality or the same and they are 25-30% cheaper.

Don't' start a tour to shops without having programmed and written down your needs. The psychotherapy of window shopping is extremely dangerous for your wallet and the family budget. And when you get in a shop, keep your eyes only on your list and avoid the Serenes of things you may like and on "special offers" , buy what you need an ONLY that, pay (cash if possible) and get out quickly!

"Be aware of credit cards"! They are slowly burning bombs in your wallet or bag and when they explode, dismantle your budget and your family. Stop immediately their credit function. That is don't charge them with amounts bigger than the ones you can easily afford to pay at the end of the month.

Stop getting loans from your cards, your bank or -even worse-loan sharks! In short, don't ever spend more than you earn! Do not forget that excess loaning was one of the main causes of the financial crisis around European Union and not only!

Forget the often consumption of costly delicacies, like black and red caviar, champaign, lobsters, truffles, mangos and all these extravagant goodies, offered by grocery and vegetable extraordinary expensive "boutiques". Once a while, if you will dearly want them, you can buy some and you will enjoy them far more, while at the same time you will have avoided your pocket's bleeding.

Forget also the extensively expensive clothes, shoes, accessories and cosmetics, made by renowned firms. You can find and buy equally good but far cheaper products, not paying for the firm label, but just for the value of the product!.. Additionally, if you cannot live without the products of big firms, there are the stock houses. Nobody will notice that your dress or your shoes are two years old fashioned!

There is no reason at all to buy and eat fruits and vegetables off their season. They are very expensive and not so good.

In parallel you can create your own small orchard. If you don't have enough ground space, even pots will do. You can grow nearly costless tomatoes, cucumbers, eggplants, lettuces, peppers, zucchinis, mint, basil, dill, kaparai, laurel etc. and you will have personal satisfaction, pride and joy, freshness, excellent quality and taste and all that for FREE!

If it happens to have a big garden, you can also have your own fruits, like oranges, cherries, apples, tangerines, figs, apricots, peaches, melons, water melons, lemons etc.

In addition, if conditions permit it, you can also have chickens, rabbits and pigeons and eat fresh eggs and white healthy meat. If you live in the country, needless to say that you can extend your agricultural cultivation and add potatoes, beets beans, lamps, goats and even cows.

"Be aware of Chinese, even cheap products selling"! Do not be carried away by their extremely low prices. My grandmother was saying that "dogs eat the cheap meat"! Of course not all Chinese products are defective and bad and sometimes even dangerous! You can trust some reliable firms and legal shops. In any event, avoid the "black market", because you endanger your money and harm the industry and trade of your country and encourage frauds and illegal immigrants.

The same exactly goes for most of the products of the telemarketing shops. They give promises never kept and wear out within no time. This misleading advertising (save some exceptions) leads to a big waste of money.

Don't forget and don't despise the street markets. They take more labor and time, but they give in return, fresh, of good quality and less expensive goodies.

Look for, find and take advantage of the sales and special offers, advertised both on TV and conventional advertising media, as well as on internet.

Speaking about internet, you can find in general less expensive products and services. Additionally there are some sites, which make every day tremendous offers, over 50%. Here is a list of such sites, but I cannot guarantee their quality and their solvency. This is up to you to check:

e-bay.com, ricardo.gr, e-shop.gr, strawberrynet.com (cosmetics), groupon.gr, skroutz.gr, goldendeals.gr, goldenshopping.gr, me&home.gr, ricardeals.gr, goldenwin.gr, getitnow.gr, smarteconomy.gr, myhabit.com, summydress.gr.com, xestock.gr, coupeconomy.gr, buldoza.gr, tzaba.gr, petdeals.gr , cheapies.gr, stockout.gr, smartathens.gr etc.

In any case be careful with the safety of your internet transactions. There are three ways to protect yourself from hackers and find your card supercharged:

Get a credit card with low coverage e.g. €200

Pay through Paypal, if the e-shop has it

Get an "empty" charging card and charge it each time with the amount you want to pay.

Safety and Insurance

Insure all of your assets and movable goods! Insurance has not been invented for the rich, but for the poor people, who cannot afford to pay in order to restore big damages. In parallel do everything it takes to secure your movable goods from theft! Loss of goods nowadays costs far more than before the crisis both economically and psychologically!

Forget what we all believe: "This is not going to happen to me". With the criminality hitting red, it can happen to all of us, anytime, anywhere and in numerous ways.

Insurance fees are neither luxury nor waste of money. It is potentially a wise, huge and "lifesaving" investment!

Insure all sorts of buildings you have against flood, fire and earthquake.

Insure all your movable things against theft and fire.

Buy fire extinguishers, one for the kitchen (where 90% of home fires start) and one or more for the rest of the house and do not forget to recharge then once a year. The same goes for any kind of building you poses.

Don't walk around with a lot of cash on you or other valuables, like expensive watches, jewelry, i-phones, i-pads etc.

If you carry a bag or briefcase make sure you walk on the pavements close to the buildings and hold your bag or briefcase from the wall's side.

Try not to walk around dangerous areas, especially during the nights.

Be extremely careful, when you take money from your bank or ATM. It is one of the favorite places of thieves.

Put a safety door in your house, which you must always lock, even when you are in your home and especially during nights, because criminals don't hesitate to enter, even when they know you are in and in that case you endanger not only your property but also your life! Don't ever leave your keys on the door. You make it easier for the thieves to break in.

If you lose your credit cards, call immediately your bank and ask them to annul them.

Install in your house and business alarm connected with the Police or/and a Security company.

Install railings to all the possibly vulnerable doors and windows.

Take a big dog and keep it in your home, because if you leave it in the garden/yard, it is a sitting duck for the criminals since they can easily neutralize it with an anesthetic spray.

When you leave your home for quite a time, leave a radio on quite loudly and if it is night, leave on also a light, which can be seen from the street.

Do not leave on your telephone machine messages, like: "Sorry we cannot answer because we will be away for the next couple of weeks". Such messages are direct invitation to thieves to visit your house!Cars

Cars absorb a big portion of the family budget, in many ways like gas, insurance, spare parts, maintenance, traffic bills, parking cost etc.. So, there is a big area for savings.

It is not the right time for more cars per family. Keep only the absolutely necessary and sell the rest. You will save the expenses and put some extra Euros in your pocket.

Change your old big car with a new, hybrid, electric or diesel small car.

Forget beautifying your car with various extra accessories and hyperbolic maintenance. Be sure that your tires and brakes are in excellent condition and check regularly oil. These are safety factors and no money saving on them is permitted. Don't worry about small scratches on the body of the car. Consider them as an... original decoration!

Find a good, reliable, honest workshop for your car, in your neighborhood and take it there for maintenance. It will certainly cost less than in the workshop of the car manufacturer. In parallel don't use original spare parts, but credible spare parts from the free market.

Forget high speeds, abrupt starts and aggressive, silly overtaking. Be gentle with the gas pedal, like you step on a fresh egg, without breaking it!

When a driver shows his intention to overtake you, don't react like a child, increasing your speed. You put in danger his and your life and you weaken your wallet. Slow down and give him space for the sake of safety!

Turn of immediately your engine each time you stop for over three minutes.

Don't ever park illegally. It will cost far more than a parking ticket, save the trouble.

Nobody will accuse you if your car is not always shining!

If you have the necessary space and means you can clean it yourself when it gets really dirty, otherwise take advantage of the free... rain washing.

Use the cheapest suitable for your car gas and find the cheapest gas station on your usual route.

Reduce as much as possible the long journeys.

Don't overuse air conditioning or heating in your car. It consumes about 10% more gas.

Insure your car against all damages, even when you are responsible yourself. It is more expensive than the common insurance, but it can save you from big troubles and lots of money.

Drive always with your windows closed and your doors blocked in order to avoid attacks from thieves, when you stop for any reason, even before a red traffic light.

Don't ever get out of your car e.g. for buying cigarettes, leaving the keys on the engine. You make a great gift to potential thieves!

Don't ever leave exposed things in your car. They may break it in order to thieve them. Even when you drive, hide bags, briefcases and valuables under the seats.

Marriages – Birthdays – Anniversaries

During the "good days" we used to show off, with big villas, monstrous cars and luxurious receptions, in the events of marriages, birthdays or anniversaries, with hundreds of invitees, some of whom we did not even know!

We were transforming moments of personal and family joy and happiness into a public fiesta. This kind of show off was ugly even in good times. Nowadays is provocative and sinful!

The first advice may sound weird, but I think it is very serious and useful and it is dictated by the crisis. All unmarried couples should consider very seriously the possibility of getting married. It takes maturity, realism and careful weighing of their financial status and other basic parameters, both short and middle term, before they take the decision to get married, more over if they want and plan to have children soon.

If accounts are favorable, they should avoid and reject any thought of luxury and excess spending. People use to say (in order to justify respective big spending) that "Only once somebody gets married"! Beside the fact that this is not usually true (!!!), they should consider that marriage lasts a few hours, while they will live together for many years!

It is the right time to turn our thoughts and gazes at the love of our relatives and friends and forget the chase of making impression! So the organization of the marriage and a possible reception should be restricted within the real financial status of the couples and their families. It is time of love and not of show off!

The same goes for birthdays and anniversaries. Let us not waste the quality of our future life for decades for the sake of few hours!

They also should wisely plan their new home and its equipment. There is no time for big houses, expensive furniture, electric and electronic devices and gadgets and two cars! A humble financial start will offer them a serene quality of life, which they can upgrade as soon as their income permits it.

Quite few of the expenses involved in a marriage or a new born baby can be avoided, through borrowing clothes, shoes, toys from relatives or friends. A borrowed baby-form is better than not having to buy its milk!

Vacations – Excursions – Travels

Vacations, excursions and traveling are reviving and give courage to people, who face problems like the crisis we experiment and are under pressure or stress. I would say they are necessary for their psychological health. We need though to change our respective past mentality.

Reduce the yearly overall number and organize in time your vacations, excursion and trips, scattering them through the year.

Don't choose high season periods. Traveling and everything else is cheaper and more comfortable during out of season periods.

Forget traveling for long periods and to very far, exotic places.

Forget also the huge, luxurious hotels of 5 Stars. Even 2 or 3 Stars can lighten beautifully your vacations. Fortunately in all European countries and elsewhere there are small beautiful, cozy and warm lodgings, where you can enjoy your vacations or your excursions with a better quality and far cheaper than in huge hotels, where they charge you a Perrier for Dom Perpignan champaign.

Remember again the camping solution, close to nature and costless as well as the traditional picnics by lakes, rivers or in the woods.

Go after the big offers transporters and hoteliers make off season!

Forget the convoy of four cars for four couples. Two cars will do, you will enjoy the company of your friends also during driving and you will cut down to half traveling expenses and then split them in two.

Forget also your obligation to bring gifts for relatives and friends each time you are coming back home from a trip abroad.

For short excursions take with you a small car-refrigerator and put in coffee, tea, drinks, sandwiches, salads, finger-food, pies etc. You will avoid unknown and probably bad shops on your way and save quite a lot of money.

Search internet for special traveling and vacations offers, which may be 50-70% down from the normal price.

Do not despise the daily excursions near your house. We tend to go to other countries to visit interesting sites, but we despise a palace or a natural monument which are ten minutes driving from our home. Each country, each big or smaller city has a lot of monuments and beautiful nature or artificial places, worthy to visit and enjoy.

Diet

It is a common place that we get more and more obese, due to the kind of diet we have and the way we live without exercising our body, especially in big metropolitan areas. So, this area of saving is far more important for our health than the saving itself!

Our organization does not need every day meat or fish. It is just our need to satisfy our bulimia. Twice a week, one meat and one fish is more than enough for keeping our organization well fed and healthy.

Don't put too much food in your plate, because we tend to empty our plates independently of hanger. On the other hand it is a sinful way to throw away food that we did not eat. Put in your plate a reasonable for your hanger quantity and if after eating it, you feel still hungry, put some more. French say that in order to enjoy your meal and don't get indigestion, you should leave the table lightly hungry!

The Greek Mediterranean diet has been proved my numerous scientific researches the most healthy and tasty worldwide! Olive oil, vegetables, legumes, fruits, fish, white meat (chicken, rabbit, pork), plus homemade pies, sweets from fruits, white and red wines, ouzo and tsipouro can compose delicious lunches or dinners and keep your organization and your wallet healthy and strong! Forget the often consumption of weird meretricious cuisines with a lot of fat and spices. You will enjoy them far more once in a while, if you miss them for some time… And even then, choose a restaurant, with high quality, low prices and respect for their clients.

Coffee. Is interwoven with the morning awakening and. smoking! Apart from the marvelous green tea, there are a lot of healthy and tasty decoctions from various herbs (chamomile, eucalyptus, diktamo, linden, mint, sage etc.) which can satisfy your taste and your awakening and smoking needs, although it would be a great thing, if you could stop smoking.

Replace sugar with honey, where applicable, like in your coffee, tea and sweets.

Members of the family, who possibly are unemployed, can contribute in reducing family expenses, helping in many ways , like repairing small damages, cultivating vegetables, cooking and making homemade pies, ice cream, bread, cookies, cakes, sweets, beverages and many other useful things, depending on the means and the capability of the specific members of the family.etc.

Work

As already mentioned above those misfortunes that happen to be jobless can and should definitely help the family budget, in a big number of ways, depending on the needs of the family and on the dexterities of the jobless member. Delivering, baby sitting, helping old weak people, repairing small damages in their home, cooking, planting vegetables, making useful small furniture, teaching (music, gymnastics, languages and whatever they know well), jobs through internet and dozens of other things are only a few of the existing part or full time jobs, which don't ask for specific studies or dexterities and may contribute to the family's income.

Those who fortunately do have a job can reduce expenses, connected with it.

Try and find friends (or even better colleagues) who live near you and drive in the morning to the same direction with you, with whom you can share the expenses.

If it is convenient, use the public transportation means to go to your work and get long time tickets, which are quite cheaper.

Before leaving your house, put in a thermos your coffee or tea and take with you a sandwich, a piece of pie or a salad, for your lunch. They will be much taster from those of a cafeteria or snack-bar and will save you lots of money.

Each time you get your monthly salary, calculate carefully where and when you will spend it, so that you will not be penniless, before your next pay.

Management of Debts

Debts create many unpleasant implications on two mainly levels, at least for the honest, consistent and sensitive people. The first level is the purely financial one. The second is the unpleasant pressure from the lenders, inability to satisfy their demands, psychological pressure and stress. Managing debts-especially when they are far beyond our financial capacity to pay them- is really a very difficult and tough task!

The first and most important iron rule is: NO more loans! NO more debts, from any source. Loans may offer a short term relief, but they undermine the family budget and psychological serene!

Get some advice from a credible lawyer or financial consultant, regarding the possible options legislation of your country offers for settling debts to suppliers, the State or/and to Banks.

Settle up first your debts to the State. They are usually the toughest and more dangerous for your overall financial status. The State can even take your house if you don't serve your debt regularly

Banks are very willing nowadays to settle loans in your favor, by reducing the installments and prolong the time of payoff. Negotiate with them on the basis of your ability to pay the installments. It is almost certain that they will consent. They may even consent in a hair-cut of your loan.

Regarding your "soft" debts, like credits from your suppliers (for your home or your business) or/and loans from relatives and friends, speak to them openly and sincerely, ask for their understanding and agree on minimal installments for their payoff.

All creditors are always more tolerant and "softer", when they note sincerity, good will and minimal -even irregular- serving of the debt.

Clothing and Footwear

This is another big burden for the family budget, especially for those who have many… feminine members! Elegance though is one thing and show off is a completely different thing! Anybody, woman or man, can be elegant with inexpensive clothes and shoes, provided she/he has good taste. No one will esteem and respect more somebody, because he bears a label of Armani or Dior! At least not those you should be interested in… At the same time though, when you buy "labels" and not simply good and nice clothes and shoes, you empty your wallet and blow up the family budget!

Divorce fashion! It is a lethal enemy of your wallet! Your personality has nothing to lose, if your blouse is three years old and your shoes five years old.

According a Greek proverb "Black robes do not make priests", but only externally and sometimes fake! It's a shame to throw away your money, buying "robes"! If you really are a "priest", it will be obvious by your attitude in life and your mentality. If you are not, you cannot persuade people around you for a long time that you really are.

Decrease the number of clothes and shoes you buy. You are not a millipede and nobody cares if they see you after 5 days with the same dress!...

If you lack elemental clothes and shoes don't be shy and do not hesitate to ask relatives or friends to give you some, which they may not use and need.

Shoemakers and seamstresses are back in business, correcting small "accidents" and damages to shoes and clothes. Both are waiting to make "brand new" your worn out shoes or/and clothes, at nearly no cost.

With a skein of wool you can knit warm, elegant, nice wonders for the members of your family, from toes to head, again at nearly no cost.

Unless a whole bottle of red wine falls on you or you fall in a muddy pit, you don't have to send your clothes to the washing machine. There are products (spray, gel, even a small portion of your detergent) with which you can easily remove small local stains.

Your clothes do not get dirty just after 2-3 times you wear them, unless you work in a "dirty" job. Don't wear them out by washing them for no reason, because additionally you waste detergent, water and electricity.

Repair of Damages

For the last decades we used to dispose an object, in case it suffered a small or bigger damage and buy a new one, instead of repairing the old one.

You'd better forget the costly habit of buying a new thing instead of repairing the old one! The replacement of an object costs usually far more than its repair.

The electrician the carpenter the plumper of your neighborhood are very sympathetic guys and you know them for years. They usually though are not available when you need them, they don't give you a receipt for their work and they don't guarantee that what they fixed one day will work properly the next day! So you d' better call in one of the Repairing Agencies, which are reliable, consistent with time, issue receipts and give a guarantee for the work they did.

You can get a suitable, practical kit in a very reasonable price from IKEA, Praktiker, MAKRO and similar shops and repair small damages yourself. You can also find relevant "manuals" in the market and in internet to help you to make repairs and even make small furniture, like a stool, shelves, small cupboard etc. The cost is minimal and you will be proud of your ... creations!

Small Business and Free Lancers

Unemployed, retired people, small businesses and free lancers are the biggest victims of the crisis. The last two do not aim any more in making more money, but they struggle to just keep alive their business or their profession, so they can support their family.

So if your business or work faces cash flow or even more serious financial problems, the first thing you need is cold blood, psychological and sentimental distancing and realism.

The first fundamental step is to make a very careful and exact professional feasibility study of your business, on the basis of the expected in the near future pessimistic expenses and turnover, in order to see whether your business is viable or not.

The first line of defense for the survival of your business is cutting down of running expenses.

The biggest running cost of a business is usually the salaries of its employees. In small businesses though, where a small number of employees work for many years, having developed friendly or even "family" relations with the employer, it is very tough for the latter both psychologically and emotionally, to fire his collaborators. So, before deciding the last measure of firing people, he can discuss openly with his employees the decrease of their salaries or/and part time work with rotation, in order to avoid firing or even worse to shut down his business. If the employees do not consent or if the balance of expenses vs. income is negative, then firing is obligatory.

The main target though, even if the employer proceeds to firing some people is the decrease of all if possible running expenses (like rent, air condition, heating, electricity, supplies of any kind, etc.) starting from a zero basis During this procedure we must forget all of our past habits and the ways we were doing things. We have to forget what we liked to do and what was easy and convenient. The actual gnomon of our respective decisions must be one and only: to keep what is absolutely necessary for the business, aiming always at the final goal, which is to secure higher income than expenses.

Do not trust the indication of "low ink" in your printers or "low battery" in other devices, because it is always premature and…

cunning. Just have in your drawer the necessary inks and batteries and change them when they get really exhausted. If you use a lot of batteries, prefer the rechargeable ones. Additionally you can buy the "Heavy duty 6v Lantern Battery", in which you can find 30 batteries, at the price of four. Finally, you can also find cheap batteries in IKEA, Praktiker and MAKRO.

All the last years we were sort of addicted with couriers for sending out documents, letters or even small parcels. And this was done for three main reasons:

1. We were possibly delaying in doing the necessary work according our deadline and then we resorted to the speed of courier in order to catch up with the deadline.

2. There was enough money.

3. It became a wasteful habit, exactly like the cell phones vs. the conventional ones.

If we get better organized, we can use the State Post, the cost of which is nearly ten times less than courier.

Intensify your efforts for bigger sales aiming at the increase of income.

Advertising and promotion campaigns do not constitute waste! On the contrary, in times of crisis and under certain conditions, attacking the market is the best and most effective defense. We don't advertise just only business is going well, because it looks like we go to the doctor, when our health is in excellent condition! Even if you have a superb Rolls Royce, it cannot take you anywhere and it's totally useful, unless you fill its tank with gasoline! Advertising is just the necessary "gasoline" to get your business moving.

The most productive way, in order to achieve this goal is the targeted personal approach of prospective clients and the effort to persuade your already customers to increase their per capita spending.

As it is a common practice, make often attractive sales and offers and be flexible regarding payments via monthly interest free installments, through credit cards.

Make a thorough research in the market and find new lines of products or/and services. If necessary abandon your old line and get in a brand new one! Look especially for products/services, which present increased demand related to the crisis.

Given the great stiffness of Banks nowadays in loaning small business, don't you ever try to get money from loan sharks or sell a piece of land or house you have, in order to feed your business. It is a certain way towards total catastrophe, of both your business and your property!

If you happen to have loaned big amounts from Banks, it is just the right time to negotiate with them extension of the time of pay off, decrease of the installments and even hair cutting off of the total debt. They will listen to you with open ears and most possibly they will accept your terms, provided you will consistently and regularly serve your debt, even with minimal amounts.

If despite all the above numbers are not favorable, wisdom dictates closing down of the business. Successful businessman is not only the one who makes a healthy, developing and profitable business, but also he who knows when it's time to close it down! The psychological and emotional need to keep an ill business, without the necessary viable conditions and prerequisites, will most possibly lead to the death of the business, while debts will have become huge and the businessman will go to a mad house or commit suicide!

Make a research within the sector of the line of your business, for possible mergers. Unification of business entities has been proved a positive practice and not only in crisis periods. Even more then! Merging of 2-3 businesses of the same sector decreases expenses and increases turn over. It will only take abandoning of our egoism and the wish we nearly all have to be the "one and only boss" and do whatever we like, without any kind of control from anybody!

If you proceed to a merger be very careful regarding the partners you will choose and never-never make an oral agreement, even if your partner is your honest, good willed, trustworthy and beloved brother. Especially then! This is not because people are de facto fraud. There are though four objective and realistic reasons which dictate the necessity of a written agreement in any case.

Usually we hear what we want to hear and not what was actually said.

There are very often communication gaps. Somebody says something and the other understands something different.

Then memory comes. Very often people tend to forget what was really and finally agreed, especially when a lot of negotiations have taken place before the final agreement and if this agreement has quite a few conditions and rules.

There is a possibility that some of the initial partners changes, which means that the new one was not present when the agreement was being formed.

So, for some or more of the above reasons, doubts, differences and fights begin, the partnership is dismantled and probably -more important- so are relative or friendly relationships.

If the object of your business is suitable, try to open new markets abroad. Turkey and Balkan countries offer good opportunities this period.

And do not forget that in periods of crisis attack is the best defense.

Hobbies

Hobbies except for filling empty time of people with interesting and pleasant activities, offer also psychological euphoria and on top of that they can fill your wallet with their part or total liquidation, provided you have valuable collections, like art, stamps, coins etc.

On the other hand some of the hobbies are very costly, like tennis, skiing, horse riding etc.

You should manage your hobbies during the crisis on the basis of the follow axes:

Stop investing on your collections.

Start liquidating in the highest price you can get under the circumstances, part of your collections or the whole of them

Stop any subscriptions in respective clubs (tennis, horse riding etc.)

If you are a fun of cinema, music and books, internet offers a real thesaurus of all that for free. Additionally you can borrow or/and exchange books, DVD and CD with your friends.

Electricity

Electricity is an important expense of the family budget and unfortunately our whole life is depending on it. This does not mean we should work for paying electricity! We can enjoy the goodies of electricity without meaningless wastes. If you had in front of your eyes the electricity counter and see the way it rampages with unnecessary wastes, you would be terrified and definitely turn off any open without reason switches.

A radical solution would be to switch to another source of power (photovoltaic, naturals gas), which will bring down the overall cost.

Double window glasses and an overall insulation of your house will bring down your electricity bill, both in summer and winter. (Cooling and heating).

Don't leave open doors and windows, when you have on air condition or heating. Both consume far more energy, in order to heat or cool your house. You may and you should though leave slightly open one window, in both cases.

Don't change all the time degrees of the thermostat during heating or cooling your house. In winter stabilize your thermostat at 19-22 degrees and in summer at 25-28 degrees. When you change often the thermostat, you consume far more energy and money.

Buy air conditions of the last technology (inverter) which consume far less energy.

Don't forget fans. They provide pleasant coolness quietly and consume minimal energy.

Look in the market for other, more economic means of heating than the central one.

Close down air condition and heating units in rooms which you don't use.

Replace all bulbs with those of the new technology, which consume 75% less electricity.

Don't leave your electronic devices "stand buy". The additional consumption of energy is minimal, but it is completely useless.

We light the lights only of the room we are in. Each time we get out of a room, we turn of the lights. We get in we turn on. We get out, we turn of. If you insist for some days on this habit, it will become automatic movement, like turning on and of the engine of your car.

At least once a year call a technician to check, clean and maintain your air condition and your burner.

Kettle is a convenient and economical appliance. Each time you use it though, put in it as much water as you need. If you want to make tea for two, for example, just put in the kettle two caps of water. If you put a lot of water, you waste time, water and money!

If you see an electricity bill extremely high, take down the general switch and check the meter. If it runs, it means you have a leakage and throw money out of the window. In this case, call the electricity company to fix the leakage.

Electronics and Gadgets

It is true that internet and electronics have changed completely our lives offering, knowledge and communication for free and made it more convenient, faster and economic! It is also true that the electronic industry has found the way to sell us more than we really need and spend a lot of money, without getting always real "value for money".

The first way they in which they are milking our wallets is the continuous and often change of models of electronic devices, with detailed and marginal changes which make some times more difficult their usage and in any case do not worth the additional cost. As long as the "previous" model" satisfies your needs, there is no reason at all to waste money on a newer model, just to prove you are "in", unless it offers you new features and applications which you really need.

All electronic products are very sensitive and vulnerable to very high or low temperatures, to water and to crash.

The real cesspool though is i-phone, i-tablet and i-pod, which with their continuously "developed" models undermine the family budget. Get them if you really need them and don't change them like... shirts!

Nearly 90% of gadgets do not offer any quality in our life. We all can live without gadgets and with more Euros in our wallet.

Computer, printer, scanner, webcam have become necessary accessories of our life. It is nonsense though to waste money on far more powerful and bigger than our needs demand, by buying giant screens and luxurious peripherals or/and add new programs and change software every now and then.

Avoid to print documents from your computer, if you really do not need it on had paper. If you want to keep it, just archive it and organize well your files so that you can easily find it each time you need it. Each time you press the key "print", you waste ink and paper and you hurt ecology!

Additionally, if you want to print a document for your own use, print it on the blank side of an already used paper. You economize and you save a... tree!

Dust is the worst enemy of electronic devices, after coffee... poured on them! Clean often your electronic devices according to the manual of each one. So, you will not waste money on repairs and new devices.

Maintain regularly your electronic devices, because industry has arranged that repair costs nearly as much as a new device.

Social Expenses

It is very nice to offer gifts. And very selfish! That's why we tend to buy gifts we would like for ourselves and not for the recipients... Despite that, we feel noble and generous each time we give a present offering joy to the recipient or... obliging him/her! Of course there are also the innocent, without second thoughts

gifts from pure love, but these are fewer. Nevertheless both kinds of gifts are a luxury in a period of crisis.

We also feel "lords" inviting friends in our home for a Luculian dinner or buy them a dinner in a restaurant, ordering the most expensive dishes and wines.

Cut down gifts. Offer to those whom you really love or to whom you are grateful for their support.

Offer simple gifts of love, sympathy and interest. The proof of all three does not lie on the price of the gift, but on the thought, the pain and the care, with which you found it or –even better- made it yourself!

A book, a flower, a handmade jewelry or decorative item from shells are more precious gifts, which witness your love far more intensively and convincingly than any expensive and impersonal gift.

Don't underestimate a simple warm phone call on birthdays, name days, Christmas and anniversaries or a specially designed e-mail by you for the recipient.

If you chose though to send or give a gift, don't ever forget to accompany it with a warm wishing card, mentioning also the date. If the card is addressed to a relative or close friend and it is your professional one, don't forget to strike off your professional title and NOT your name, as many people do by mistake.

A gift gets great additional emotional value if it bears (printed, engraved or even knitted) the name or the initials of the recipient. It is almost costless and makes your gift unique.

Get rid from the silly social compulsion, according which it's a shame to offer a gift, which was initially offered to you. If you receive a gift, which you already have or it is useless for you or you simply don't like it you may certainly give it to somebody else, who could appreciate it. Just take care though to remove from it any wishing card addressed to you or/and change the... Christmas packaging if you offer it in midsummer! If somebody "accuses" you for improper attitude, just ask him: "What if someone donated me as a gift a Rolls Royce, which I did not want and offer it to you? Would you still characterize this offer as "improper"?...

Besides exceptional cases, put an end in paying the bill of a restaurant yourself alone! Let's go back to the old good habit, when each one was paying his share, women included, by dividing the bill "per capita".

When you invite friends to your house you don't have to prove them you are rich. They now very well where you are standing financially. A starter, a simple every day dish, a common wine and a fruit, is more than enough for a pleasant evening among friends.

On the other hand when you go to a friend's house invited for dinner, you don't have to carry a two pounds cake or a 25 years old whisky. A bottle of wine or a few flowers is more than enough to prove your friendly and gentle attitude. If your friends know your situation, be sure they welcome you even with empty hands.

Moving Around

A great part of our resources (time, money, psychological sereni-ty) is being spent on moving around. We have to change the way we were moving around until today.

Remember the two marvelous tools nature has given us, our legs. They offer us free moving and walking is very good for our health and our wallet. Let's forget that even when we were using our cars we were struggling to find a place to park exactly outside the door of our destination, lest we walked for 50 meters.

The second less costly and healthy mean is bicycle. It is fun, cov-ers more easily and faster greater distances and it's also good for our health.

Let's get again aboard the public transportation means (subway, buses, trams, even taxis). They are cheap, sometimes faster than private cars, safe and offer psychological serenity. Mind you to buy the even cheaper tickets of monthly, multiple routes and means. Besides saving we also help environment.

You can avoid a lot of movements for shopping, using internet, where you can find almost anything you want, buy it and have it brought to your house. You save labor, time, gasoline and parking tickets. On top of that and especially for super markets, according researches, when you go there you buy 25-30% more of the prod-ucts in your list or those you really need. Just send a mail, a fax or make a phone call and your goodies (and only the ones you need) will be delivered free at your home.

If for some movements (work, friendly meetings, outing in the evening etc.) you cannot avoid driving, try to find friends, neigh-boring with you, who are going to the same place or to the same direction use one car at a time and share gasoline.

The same exactly combination goes for vacations and excursions. It is real nonsense to get two cars for two couples, while you can cut expenses down to 50%, split it in two and enjoy your friends' company also during driving.

Even for professional meetings, instead of spending a fortune in trips and hotels, you can arrange telephone or video teleconferences and save a lot of time, trouble and money.

Water

Sun, oxygen and water are the three elements of nature on which the lives of all living beings are depended. The first two are for free. The price of the third has surpassed this of oil! So, economizing on water is important for the family budget.

Abolish or reduce the frequency of taking baths in a full bathtub. Shower does exactly the same job, but with much less water. If you close the bathtub siphon and take a long, enjoyable shower, you will see that the water will cover only 2-3 centimeters of the bathtub. Great economy!

Don't leave faucets to run like hell, while you are brushing your teeth, shaving or washing your hands. Low flow of the water is not only more convenient it is also very economic.

Get rid from the "fabricated" social compulsion, according which you HAVE to take a bath EVERY day! It's not a health issue. Nobody gets dirty within a few hours or 2-3 days, unless his job is dirty or he sweats during hot summer days. Take a bath whenever you really feel like or/and the conditions of your life and work ask it and not whenever the social compulsion dictates it.

The same exactly above goes for washing your hair.

The toilet water tank is the most consuming water thing. Daring suggestion: when you go to the toilet for only hydraulic reasons, DO NOT press the flush! Just thing of saving the cost of 60-240 of water tanks per month, depending on the number of the family members! If this solution sounds extreme to you, put in the water tank two big bricks.

If you have a garden or pots in your veranda and balconies, install automatic watering system. It is quite inexpensive, it secures the regular watering, it is far more economic than the manual watering and saves you from the trouble to find somebody to water your plants, every time you are away for some days or on vacations.

Don't use every now and then your washing machine for 2-3 clothes, because you want your dearly dirty turquoise blouse, your new dirty yellow shirt or your multicolor bermouda. Wait until you gather a good volume of dirty clothes in order to exploit the total capacity of your washing machine, saving thus on water, detergent and electricity.

If you use the economic and convenient electric kettle, fill it with as much water as you need each time e.g. two cups of water for two cups of tea. It boils faster and you consume less water and electricity.

If your home is not a... hotel or transit spot, there is no reason at all to change sheets and towels every now and then. They wear out and you waste lot of water, detergent, electricity and labor for washing them and ironing them! A reasonable time of change is every 10-15 days.

Don't overdo it with the washing of windows glasses, verandas and balconies. Of course you must keep your house clean, but it is not necessary that it shines every day! A few stains on your windows or some fallen leafs on your veranda do not obscure the cleanliness of your house. And do not forget that the rain has the habit to fall the next day you cleaned your windows!...

Children

I believe that children are not born rude, lazy or selfish. Children inherit from their parents basically health and mind. So the behaviors and attitudes of children are acquired by the treatment from their parents and their school and especially from what they see and not from what they hear!

Parents usually like to say they sacrifice their lives for their kids benefit. This is true only when they really make sacrifices for satisfying fundamental needs of their children, like housing, feeding, clothing and education. When they rush though to satisfy all demands of their children, even the most extreme ones, they really satisfy themselves, harming at the same time severely the character of their kids.

So, the follow suggestions refer more to the proper breeding of a child for its own good and secondary on the involved economic factor.

If you ask any children psychologist, he will tell you that kids, like dogs, need the leash, because they feel secure. The leash doesn't mean a continuous tight control on kids or total refusal by the parents to any wish of their children. It means positive guidance through life.

It is possible that a family which faces a serious financial problem will have to say more times NO or DON' T to their children. Before that though they have to explain to them WHY they say NO. Children should not be isolated from life, no matter how unpleasant the situation is. Offering them goodies beyond family's financial ability, teaches them that they will always get what they want. They will find themselves though in a very unpleasant and difficult position when they will find out that society does not function exactly this way... Just the opposite! And they will not be prepared to face this reality.

Schools do basically two things: they teach mathematics and literature and they shape characters of future citizens. The mixture of the pupils of the public schools is far closer to the mixture of the overall population, than that of private schools. In that sense, personally I would choose the first, if I had children, for a simple reason. I believe that a child living in a more realistic environment which reflects society forms a better character as a citizen. And I also believe that a good character is far more important than knowledge, taking into consideration that a child that wants to learn will do it independently of his environment, public or private school. And we should not overcome the economic positive side effect of choosing a public school.

Additional knowledge or/and skills on top of those the school offers are not necessary, unless a child shows an exceptional talent in music, dancing, painting, sports, architecture etc. when of course it must be helped and fully supported to cultivate and work on this talent. The general tendency though that all children must learn dancing or piano and do sports is wrong. There are international researches which prove that children are the harder working people on the planet. It is pedagogically wrong to push and press children, depriving them from their childhood and their playing hours which are oxygen for them. Again the financial aspect of this comes second, but it is important.

The pocket money parents and relatives give to children and teenagers is something which can spoil them or teach them, what money and its management means and make them responsible for their lives. Parents who satisfy extreme demands of their children mostly do it for their own sake and really prepare irresponsible citizens, who will not be able to face effectively the difficulties of real life outside the protective walls of their parents. On the contrary, it is a very healthy and educative way if a family arranges, with the agreement of their children a standard monthly amount of pocket money, tailored to the family's financial ability and to the real needs of a child in relation with his age and the parameters of his life. IN NO CASE at all though, should they give additional money if the child or the teenager has spent all his pocket money by the 20th of the month!... This way children and teenagers learn how to use money, they understand that money is not endless, they acquire the sense of responsibility and they take their lives in their hands. Even better is when an increase of the amount of pocket money or an extra present is being connected with some achievement , like "If you get "A", I will buy you an i-phone"! Here, the financial bet is far bigger, but again it comes second to the values and principles planted to the young minds.

Gifts and toys parents, relatives and friends donate to kids play an important role in building their character for which many children psychologists believe that it is completed at the age of six years. In this sense, if kids get violent toys they will become violent. If they get a lot of expensive toys and gifts, they will become consumer freaks and greedy. If they get though books they will love reading and if they get musical CD's they will love music. Choose few, simple and if possible educative gifts and toys, according to family's financial ability, which will give them joy and at the same time they will sharpen their mind or their talents, like painting, constructions etc. And again you will have a positive financial side effect.

Give a homemade snack to your children for their school. You secure quality and you save money.

Don't dress your children with in fashion branded clothes and don't load them with expensive watches, i-phones, i-tablets. You "educate" them wrongly about the real values of life and you may instigate jealously from their schoolmates. Keeping a simple but aesthetic and elegant dress code for your children, you save also money.

Even better, use for your kids clothes shoes and items from your elderly kids. If you don't have, don't hesitate to borrow from relatives and friends. Children do not know the difference between new and well used clothes, shoes or toys, provided you will package and present them in a nice way, not hiding of course the truth.

Children parties are positive events because they cultivate sociability and offer the opportunity to start building friendships, which mostly are for life. These parties though should not be used as a means of show off of the family' riches! Kids are not interested at all if food is caviar and salmon or ham and tuna fish or/and –even better- homemade delicacies

The only thing they want is to have fun! And they also don't need professional entertainers for that. Table games and social interaction games, music and dance are more than enough to make kids feel good and have lots of fun. Don't spoil your kids and their friends and safeguard your wallet.

Face and Body Care

Huge are the amounts of money spent for buying products and services for the care of face and body, in the cosmetics industry, the various institutes and Gyms. The champions in this "sport" are definitely women, but recently men have started competing with them in this area.

If we exclude products and services of this sector which are good for the health of face and body, all the rest are luxurious and needless expenses, which should be cut immediately, while the crisis lasts. If we abstain from those for a few years, the quality of our lives will not be decreased at all while our wallet will be substantially increased!

Nobody will suffer from withdrawal syndrome if we decrease the frequency of beautifying our face, our hair and our body.

Nobody really needs three hydrating crèmes for the face and another three for the eyes, twelve lipsticks, six mascaras, five different shampoos, eight different perfumes and four shaving foams. It is an extremely costly habit.

It is certainly good, healthy and beautiful to have a slim body and not carrying needless pounds. Pounds though don't leave with just everyday visits to sliming institutes and gyms, while at the same time we sit all day motionless in a chair or sofa watching TV and eating all the time junk food and fat! If we take good care of our diet and exercise a little ourselves every day for 10-20' minutes, pounds will leave from your body and Euros will stay in your wallet.

Women can certainly be beautiful and attractive, without visiting each week a hair stylist and change the length, the shape and the color of their hair.

We all know and can cut and treat our nails ourselves. There is no need at all to pay for this. Additionally, psychedelic painting of women's nails can wait until the end of the crisis.

Decorating our body with tattoo and piercing can also wait until the end of the crisis, losing not even one grammar of our life's quality.

Don't apply three centimeters of toothpaste on your toothbrush! Even half a centimeter will do the job. Your aim is to clean your teeth and not fill your mouth with foams and empty quickly the toothpaste tube!

I really don't know if the slogan regarding washing teeth "First thing in the morning and last in the evening" is a marketing trick or a real healthy habit. I suspect it is the first one. In any case, ask your dentist...

Boats

Boats even the small ones don't consume only gasoline or petrol. They consume in many ways many Euros, with their maintenance, the port fees, personnel, taxes etc. like for example hosting friends.

Get rid of any boat you have. Sell it even at a low price, getting rid of the expenses and putting some Euros in your pocket.

If you want and you CAN keep it, then try and find a cheap port.

Cut down the long journeys.

Sail with reasonable speed, consuming less fuel.

Fire personnel that is not necessary for sailing.

If your boat has a small kitchen, fill up your refrigerator with food and drinks, avoiding thus to spend your money in various shops with questionable quality and high prices.

House

The rent alone of a house absorbs about 25-30% of the family budget, while those who have their own house spend 15-20% of their budget for its maintenance. When the spending is big, there is also a big margin for saving money.

Negotiate with your land lord a lower rent. In times of crisis like this one, when prices of real estate are "demolished", all house owners are positive to negotiations for a lower rent, because they know that if you leave they might not find a new tenant. It is clearly a win-win situation.

If you have your own house, see that you decrease its running cost, by installing isolating features and a more economical source of energy.

If your house is big for your current needs (because your children left for studies or got married for example), rent a smaller one and if it is yours, sell it and buy a smaller and more convenient one. In this case don't become slaves of furniture and other objects, like shoes, clothes, records, decorative items, for which there is no probably enough space in the new, smaller house! Things are made to serve people and not the opposite! Take with you the things you really need and love and get rid of the rest with one of the ways you will find in chapter "Useless an unnecessary movable things"

Don't be carried away by the "glamorous" areas, where prices of houses are sky rocketing. There are excellent houses in less glamorous areas, at far lower prices.

If you move to a new house, see that it is close to your work or/ and close to a subway station. You will save time and money. Our free time has been dramatically reduced. Let's not waste what has been left from it going back and forth to our work. It may sound weird but it's true: physical and psychological weariness ends up also to financial waste, because we lose hours of productive work, of rest, of sleep, even of entertainment, all necessary for a good health and less money spent for doctors and medicines.

Consider seriously the possibility to move in a smaller town or even village. Cost of life there is far lower from big towns and cities and the consuming temptations far less. On top being close to nature and the lack of stress offer a much better quality of life.

Time for roommates, relatives or friends, splitting thus expenses, which anyway will be decreased even only by not paying two rents, plus heating, electricity, washing machine, food etc. In parallel people will get closer and remember the days of friendship, warmth and solidarity. Just because though living together under the same roof asks for retreats and compromises plus losing time and space privacy, we must chose very carefully the people with whom we will decide to live with and agree on a minimum level of understanding each one's needs and habits.

Get dressed warmly in your house during winter and lower the average of temperature you used to have. Most important, keep a standard temperature at 18-22 C degrees. Closing completely down heating and reopening it costs far more than keeping a standard temperature continuously.

Look in the market for alternative solutions of heating, like heat accumulators, energy fireplaces, natural gas etc.

Isolate your home as much as you can and save a lot of money for heating and cooling it.

Remember the quite, economical, healthy and effective ceiling fans.

If you have a house domestic maid, negotiate with her, her salary. In parallel you can decide to do yourself some of the house keeping jobs (prepare breakfast, wash dishes, take garbage down to the street bucket, use the washing machine, cook now and then) and reduce the days and hours of her services.

Recycling of paper, glass, plastic and aluminum is not only a fundamental duty of citizens, if you organize it, you can also put some money in your wallet, by delivering them to recycling companies.

Do not trust the indications of "low ink" or "low batteries" on your devices. Just have ready the proper ink tubs and batteries and change them only when they really get exhausted.

Sanitas foil and Sanitas wrap are very convenient products for many different jobs. You may use them though more than once, when they don't get dirty from their first use.

You don't have to use expensive paper napkins for everyday use. A piece of the kitchen paper will do the same job and even better and save you some money.

If you have a small garden or a veranda with pots, cultivate vegetables. You will enjoy really tasteful, healthy products and save a lot of money.

Don't ever throw away excess or surplus food. Keep it in the fridge and eat it a couple of days later or use it to cook something else. It's waste of money and sinful!

Forget delivery, both because of the junk food and spending money.

I know the fond love some people have for their pets and I absolutely respect it, especially for the lonely people. Nevertheless they imply a quite important spending. Their food, their medication, their illnesses, their "hostels", when you have to go away and you cannot leave them with a relative or a friend. Their company, love and devotion are really precious, but in case the family budget cannot afford the respective expenses, you must consider it seriously…

Gambling

International researches have proven that the poorer the people the more they gamble. It is natural in a way for somebody to try and get out of poverty, through gambling. The final result though is that he gets poorer by gambling. The chances are so limited for somebody to win the roulette, black jack, slot machines, poker, bets, lotteries etc. that they waste money, hope and soul, believing they can solve their problem this way, while actually they make it bigger.

Stay away, as far as you can, from gambling! I mean systematic, passionate gambling. If somebody buys two lottery tickets per year, just to offer himself a little hope, it's not a crime.

Innumerous people have lost all their fortune and others "invest" in gambling their rent or the bread of their children! And then they get money from loan sharks, a mathematically certain way to bankruptcy or suicide!

Gambling DOES NOT solve financial problems. It makes them far worse and finally impossible to solve!

Telephone

Get rid of the bad and extremely expensive habit of abusing cell phone. Saving for some professions (like doctor, lawyer, plumper etc.) cell phone was invented for urgent, short communication. It is not the right tool for long serious professional discussions, for personal quarrels or for gossip! And never-never when you are driving! And it was not invented definitely for taking pictures and shooting videos! Go back to your conventional phone, which under certain contracts with telephone companies is completely free and use your cell phone only in cases there is an urgent need.

Remember that most of the allegedly "urgent" situations are actually not urgent. A wise friend of mine told me once "There are no urgent things. There are people who are in a hurry and live always under a permanent stress". Don't become one of those!

Carry always your cell phone with you DEACTIVATED and open it only when you have a real need to communicate, like for example to announce you will be late in an appointment or you lost your way or/and the address of your destination.

Stay away from the gadget technology, which dictates you to change your cell phone every two months with a new model.

It is extremely rude to have your cell phone activated when you are with friends at friends' houses or in restaurants and carry on long talks, while the rest stay silent and look at you awkwardly embarrassed...

Smoking

Abuse of smoking is very bad for health. Now it is also very bad for your wallet! An average smoker "burns" about € 200-300 per month! Unacceptable amount for a meager family budget!

For the sake of your health first and secondly for the sake of your pocket, stop immediately smoking, cigarettes, cigars or pipe!

If you are not strong enough to cut smoking, try the electronic harmless cigarette (as European Commission recently stated), which may also facilitate you to gradually stop real smoking.

If you smoke an expensive brand, try another less expensive.

Do not let ashtrays smoke your cigarettes...

Try to reduce the number of cigarettes you smoke gradually, by two less cigarettes per day, until you reach... zero!

Health – Medicines

It would never ever cross my mind to suggest any sort of economy related with health issues! There are though some hyperboles in handling our health and our medication, which are really harmful firstly for our health itself and then for our wallet.

There are some people, who consciously refuse to pay a visit to a doctor or use medicines. Others visit doctors often without reason and swallow tenths of pills every day. Both attitudes are very dangerous for health! The second one is also very dangerous for your financial health!

Regarding the second category of hypochondriacal people, a wise friend of mine used to say: "There was a time that doctors made their living from the ill people. Now they get rich from the healthy people"!

Take good care of your health and take all the necessary preventive examinations, depending on your sex and your age, like mammography, Pap Test, PSA etc. Prevention is not only the best way to a good health it is also far more economic!

It's never a good time for illnesses. Much more now, within a financial crisis, which on one hand makes it difficult to get the right treatment and on the other it deprives the family budget from precious resources and from income, since ill people cannot work! Protect yourself even from light colds, which may evolve to serious illnesses. Get rid from anxiety and stress, in the degree this is humanly feasible, because these are the main causes of innumerous (if not all!) illnesses.

In case you have even a simple symptom, like cough which though insists, visit immediately a pathologist. He is the right doctor to make the first diagnosis and then send you to a specialist, if necessary.

Do NOT ever "play the doctor" and make arbitrary diagnosis yourself or with the aid of "wise" friends or through internet and remember that sometimes the same exactly symptoms, have a quite different cause and hide a totally different illness.

Chose ONE doctor, whom you trust and don't waste precious time and money "touring" to various different doctors, buying opinions, which very often clash each other and cause you confusion and insecurity.

On the other hand don't become hypochondriacal and rush to doctors every now and then and with the lightest symptom.

You should never live on… medicines. Medicines are not meals! Don't ever take medicines without your doctor's prescription and don't take larger doses than those he advised you.

Even the most innocent medicine has in some cases unpleasant repercussions. In parallel, when you abuse medicines your organism gets used to them, causing decrease of their effectiveness. Like mosquitoes, which after being over rinsed with DDT, made it their favorite… drink! Remember: POLYFARMACY is very bad both for your health and your wallet!

Do not stock quantities of medicines, which you really do not need, in case you will need them some time in the future. The most possible is that they will expire before you need them and you will have to throw them away, along with some Euros.

Province

Life is very different in the province. It has definitely better quality fewer temptations and fewer expenses! If you can go and live there do it immediately.

As for the permanent inhabitants of province like farmers, professionals, owners of small business etc., most of the above saving measures referring to inhabitants of cities and towns apply also to them.

Channel all of your energy in improving your agricultural or/and kettle production both in quantity and mainly in quality. Leisure is nowadays a big waste,

Check and maintain properly all your mechanical and professional equipment, in order to avoid repair expenses, save energy cost and improve your production.

Devote additional time in taking good care of your plant and animal capital.

Take advantage and exploit the innovative techniques and means of high technology, increasing your productivity.

Search and apply innovative cultivations, which may ask for more work and care but they bring very good money.

Decrease your trips to big cities and abroad.

Tips

Tipping is a gentle and generous gesture. In difficult times though it may become a luxury for the family budget! And since nearly all incomes have been reduced, it is imperative to reduce tips, if not cut them completely! If you decide to give a tip though, remember three things:

You are struggling to save, due to the decrease of your income and this is a painless saving..

Many restaurants, bars hotels etc. include in their bills a certain "tipping" percentage for their personnel.

Don't ever give a tip to somebody who doesn't worth it, as to a lazy and rude waiter.

Entertainment

If you take a good look in your "Table of expenses" (an imperative tool for saving, as it is mentioned in the beginning of this book), you will find out that the entertainment expenses absorb a good portion of your income. Of course a reasonable entertainment is a psychological crosier, especially for people who face problems and are anxious and stressed. "Metron Ariston" (Measure is optimum) the ancient Greeks used to say! Apply this principle everywhere and to your entertainment.

Forget often outing! One outing per week is enough to give you a pleasant break from your problems.

Forget all "high class" and "in" restaurants and clubs, where people usually go just for show off. There are a lot of excellent restaurants, clubs and tavernas, even in your neighborhood, which respect their clients and offer, cozy environment, excellent food, good service, at very reasonable prices.

When you go out to a restaurant order skimpy and not for feeding a whole battalion! If your initial order will not be proved adequate, make an additional order. It is unacceptable though to leave behind a table full of food. It is not only a big waste it is also socially provocative and bad for your health and your wallet. Restrict your gluttony for the sake of both. French say that "You must leave the table slightly hungry", in order to enjoy what you ate, not discomfort your stomach and not get additional pounds!

Avoid often consumption of "elaborated" expensive dishes for money reasons and junk food for health reasons. A simple dish well cooked with pure and fresh ingredients may offer you the same joy as a lobster.

Don't do it ALL in one evening! Some people go to theatre, then to a restaurant and end up in a club or bar. Chose one kind of entertainment each time. It will give you the joy you need and it will save you money. And don't forget anyway, that the best enjoyment is a good company!

Arrange evenings with a simple dinner, rotated among friends' houses. You can even arrange "joures fix" at each one's house.

When you are invited a t a friend's home you don't have to show him how... rich you are, by carrying a three pounds cake or a 25 year old whisky. A bottle of wine or a few flowers are more than enough! They will not love or respect you less if they are real friends. And if they are not, just don't bother! Real friends will not bother even if you go with empty hands!

Movies and theatre offer excellent and inexpensive outing.

If you like walking or/and biking, I am sure there are a lot of nice places near you, where you can spend your weekends and enjoy natural or/and artificial beauties, with good company and practically no money. Parks, groves, lakes, rivers, zoos, seashores, mountains, caves, ancient monuments and other worth to see and enjoy natural or artificial spots can make your day!

Make sure that in these short excursions you take with you in a small icebox coffee, tea, water, sandwiches, salads and finger food.

Picnic used to be a very popular form of entertainment, for families, friends, relatives and couples in love. Bring them back in your life.

Stop expensive subscriptions to magazines and newspapers, since you can get free in internet all the updated information and entertainment you want.

Stop expensive subscriptions to any kind of clubs of which you are probably a member.

Enjoy quiet, cozy, evenings at home, with family, relatives and/ or friends, playing cards, table games (do not forget that even the older people hide a kid inside them) or watching TV, with home-made finger food and NOT pizza or other delivery junk food.

ADDITIONAL INCOME

The second important factor for facing effectively the crisis, is to try and get some additional income. Of course in times of deep financial crisis this is not easy at all, but it's worth trying! Just sitting down, crying and cursing, full of anger and despair will not solve any problem. It is like you have put your head in a guillotine and wait for the blade to drop!...

Before start looking for a job it is imperative to leave behind our knowledge, diplomas, abilities, talents, dexterities, experience and –most of all- the height of our compensations before the crisis. If we manage to get rid from these prejudices and taboos and keep wide open our eyes and our mind, we will manage to find far easier a job. ANY JOB, since the "Managing Directors" positions simply do not exist!

Some indicative jobs are, baby sitting, dog walking, taking care of old people, household aiding, farming, taxi driving, delivery etc. There are always thousands of classified jobs among which he/she who wants really to work will find one.

There is also a good variety of jobs offered in internet, for part time or full time occupation.

If you chose internet, be aware of fraud offers and check very carefully the reliability and integrity of the organization behind them. Very often they over promise and ask for an "joining fee" which you don't know where it will lead you while there is a good possibility to lose it!...

Forget all past excuses, like "I don't like this job", "it's inferior to my abilities and personality", "it is far from my home", "the boss is rude", "the salary is low" etc., etc. Any job –and I mean ANY JOB- is better than hunger or begging...

Finally unemployed members of the family, instead of hanging around drinking coffee and beer, can help cutting down the family budget, by contributing to the maintenance of the household, washing dishes, cleaning, cooking, gardening, repairing small damages etc., etc.

Realty

Some people, especially those over 60 face with a weird way their financial problem. While they own a number of houses, shops and land, prefer to "make their life difficult", instead of selling or even "killing" some of them in order to improve their life quality. It is a major double fault: they pay a lot of money in taxes and maintenance, while they could get rid of them and put some good money in their pockets.

At this point I would like to express a purely personal opinion. If we except the homeless and the really poor people, I believe it is less painful for somebody to have lived his whole life on a budget of let's say € 3.000 on which he continues to live, than those who were living on a budget of € 4.500 and now they are obliged to cut down their budget by € 1.500 cutting probably "luxurious" habits, which though were for decades an integral part of their lives.

Those lucky ones who happen to have some realty , which instead of bringing them today some income absorbs part of it in taxes and maintenance and face a cash flow problem, should liquidate part of it (never the whole of it), even at very low prices, in order to ensure a better life quality.

We must all realize and understand that the prices of all goods and services we knew in countries which are in crisis, simply DO NOT EXIST! The total market has balanced on a far lower level than that before the crisis, dictated by the iron market law of "offer and demand" and there is nothing anybody can do to change that short term.

The right philosophy I believe behind the above suggestion is that bricks and stones cannot offer a life quality. We keep only those necessary for future financial security.

Useless and Unnecessary Movable Things

If you take a careful, cool look around your house, you will discover a great lot of really useless and unnecessary things, which you would not miss at all, if they were not there! You most probably would not even notice their absence. In some houses there are three sets of cutleries, four sets of dishes 36 pieces each, tenths of small and bigger decorative items, small pieces of furniture the only service they offer is that they occupy space, books that will never be reread, records which will never be rehear, tenths of costumes, dresses and shoes, seven watches, four TV sets, pounds of small silver items and jewelry, some of which found roof in your house gradually through the years, sometimes even without your will, as presents for example.

The quality of your life will not decrease the least, if you get rid of most of them!

The big problem is to manage and take emotional distance from some of them, which may be connected with beloved persons or important moments of your life, defeat the feeling of ownership and the subconscious thought that you may need something useless now in the future! Remember: don't become slaves of things, because "Thing are made in order to serve people and not vice versa"!

The second problem is in which way you will get rid of them, from the moment you will decide to do so! There are two ways basically: to sell them or/and to give them away to people who need them.

The more tiresome but fast way to sell everything you really don't need is to go to flee markets, having with you descriptions and photos of the items you want to sell. You can also find junk dealers to visit your house and negotiate with them on the spot.

The second easier but time consuming way is to load the items you want to sell on e-bay or/and other similar sites, with excellent photos and detailed descriptions.

Don't forget to look in your warehouses and lofts. Usually they hide forgotten "thesaurus", which can bring you good money.

If some of your items do not have remarkable value or you will not manage to sell them, donate them away to people they need them. Just make sure that they will go to people really in need and not be embezzled by crooks.

Saving - Securing of Savings

Independently of the shrinkage of a family's income, there is always even a tiny margin for savings, like € 1-5 daily. While it will not affect the overall family budget, it is a beneficial habit which helps in changing attitude vs. money and it may help in an emergency in the future.

Even more precious is to teach children to save, educating them in the real value of money and the right way to use it. Persuade your children to put aside even € 0,10 daily and now and then put yourself some coins in their money box, giving them practically a good example.

If some people were so wise or lucky and have saved some money, they have to safeguard them like the apple of their eye and don't spend them on everyday needs, like entertainment, clothes, cosmetics, jewelry etc.

Safeguarding your savings does not mean to hide them in a vase of flour or in your mattress! There are many ways to do this, increasing in parallel your capital even marginally.

The old saying "No one has lost investing on land" is still valid, especially within this crisis when prices of realty have dropped dramatically in some cases. If you decide though to invest your savings in land, you must be absolutely sure that you will not need them midterm (5-10 years).

You can find innumerous offers in internet, in traditional "classified advertising" and with the aid of reliable and credible real estate agents, using all three above methods.

Apart the urban areas don't overlook the peripheral ones even in the country. Don't take any decision though before you see with your own eyes the land, the house or the shop you would like to buy.

In case you will make your final choice, be careful and examine thoroughly, with the help of a lawyer or/and notary the official ownership titles.

Stock market, funds and foreign currencies is another option of investing your savings. In this case though you definitely need the advice of a credible expert.

Insurance agencies offer also interesting investing programs. Choosing the right one for you will need again the advice expert.

The most common and simple method is the traditional deposit in a Bank after you select s healthy, reliable bank and a program with good interest, which though will permit you to draw money from your account any time you need them.

EPILOGUE

Some of the above advices may sound annoying, difficult to apply, even weird or shocking, depending on the character, the environment and the way of life of each reader. Thus I don't expect all the readers to agree with all of my suggestions.

I do believe though firmly that in this book there are some principles, values, attitudes and habits which we should follow always, even within a healthy financial environment. And let's not forget that some of the above bad habits created or at least contributed to the crisis we now suffer.

One thing is for sure: crisis is also an opportunity to get back to eternal principles and values, forgetting the extremely materialized world in which we lived the last decades and put again in the centre of our lives MAN and human attitudes!

CURRICULUM VITAE

Who is Thalis P. Coutoupis

Born: Athens, 1941. Divorced.

Studies: Political and Economical Sciences and Law, Athens University.

Speaks fluently English.

Career

Journalism: Editor, columnist and editor in chief in Athenian dailies and magazines, 1958-67. "Express" financial daily, 1974-81. Since 1982, he comments on communication, political and social issues, in "Marketing Week".

Advertising: Co-Managing Director of the then 4th bigger Advertising Agency "Interad" S.A, 1974-82. Chairman and Managing Director of "Leo Burnett" Advertising, 1980-86, when he resigned to follow a free-lancer career, as Communication Consultant.

Public Relations: Managing Director of the then biggest P.R. Agency "Interpress" Ltd, 1968-80. Special P.R. Advisor to the then ruling party of "New Democracy", 1978-79.

Communication Manager of the same party, 1987-89. Free-lancer Communication Consultant, 1986-today. President of the Board for the National Communication Abroad, of the then ruling party PASOK, 1997-98. Member of the Board of Directors of the biggest technological institution of Greece, Athens TEI (Dec. 2012). Special Advisor to the Foreign Affairs Minister, Mr. D. Avramopoulos (Jan. 2013)

Pioneer in Corporate Communication

Pioneer in political communication, has designed and executed, since 1974, dozens of political and social campaigns, on behalf of parties, public and private organizations, institutions and individual politicians.

Considered as one of the very few specialists on Choregia (Sponsorship).

He teaches Public Relations, Advertising and Choregia, since 1971, in Universities, public and private organizations.

Has participated in numerous local and international congresses, as speaker.

Hundreds of articles and interviews of TPC have been published in Print and he is often hosted in talk shows on political, public relations, advertising, tobacco and choregia issues by Electronic Media.

Works

"Applied Public Relations", 1974 . Advertising and its Secrets", 1986 . "Choregia: Practical Guide", 1996. "Scorpion had horoscope Gemini", novel, 2002. «God had no objection", novel, 2005. "Trilogy of Commercial Communication – Public Relations, Advertising, Choregia", 2006. "Count down", novel, 2007. "Fingerprints" comments on political and social issues for the decade 2000-2009, December 2009. "282 simple ways to face economic crisis", 2013.

Additionally, he has published as Editor in Chief the following:

"Who's Whos": "Greek Who's Who", 1966. "Greek Ex-Patriots", 1971. "Alumni of American College", 1976-80. "Alumni of Moraitis School", 1990. "Business Managers", 1992. "Journalists",

1993 and 1996.

Social Activity

Member of International Public Relations Association, since 1969 and National Coordinator for Greece, 1997-99. Founder and Chairman of the "Moraitis Alumni League", (1985-87). Member of the Board of Directors of the Greek Advertising Agencies Association (1981-85), the Greek Public Relations Association and the Greek Studies Association (1978-86). Member in Meritus of the Business and Sponsorship Association (OMEPO). External Member of the Board of Directors of Athens TEI (2012 -)

Address

46, Iraklidon Street, 152 34 Halandri, Athens, Greece.

Telephone: (0030)210-685.14.10

Fax: (0030)210- 684.24.85 –

e-mail: aithalis@aithalis.gr.

Personal site (in Greek): http://www.aithalis.gr